TOTALLY GROSS HISTORY™

THE TOTALLY GROSS HISTORY OF
ANCIENT MESOAMERICA

ABBIE MERCER

rosen publishing's
rosen central®

Published in 2016 by The Rosen Publishing Group, Inc.
29 East 21st Street, New York, NY 10010

Copyright © 2016 by The Rosen Publishing Group, Inc.

First Edition

Library of Congress Cataloging-in-Publication Data

Names: Mercer, Abbie.
Title: The totally gross history of ancient Mesoamerica / Abbie Mercer.
Description: First edition. | New York, NY : The Rosen Publishing Group, Inc., 2016. | Series: Totally gross history | Includes bibliographical references and index. | Audience: Grade level 5-8.
Identifiers: LCCN 2015034332 | ISBN 978-1-4994-3762-1 (library bound) | ISBN 978-1-4994-3760-7 (pbk.) | ISBN 978-1-4994-3761-4 (6-pack)
Subjects: LCSH: Indians of Mexico--Social life and customs--Juvenile literature. | Indians of Central America--Social life and customs--Juvenile literature. | Indians of Mexico--History--To 1500--Juvenile literature. | Indians of Central America--History—To 1500--Juvenile literature.
Classification: LCC F1219.3.S6 M45 2016 | DDC 972/.01—dc23
LC record available at http://lccn.loc.gov/2015034332

Manufactured in the United States of America

CONTENTS

INTRODUCTION

How do you feel about blood? Its bright red color and metallic smell make many people a bit queasy. This would have been a huge problem if you lived in ancient Mesoamerica. Few civilizations have been as focused on blood as the Maya, Aztec, and other peoples of Mesoamerica. These cultures honored their gods with bloody human sacrifices. Many victims had their hearts ripped out. Others had their heads cut off or their skin stripped off, while still others were drowned, buried alive, thrown into wells, or shot full of arrows.

Ancient Mesoamericans also made offerings of their own blood, known as autosacrifices, to their gods. Historians think that this kind of bloodletting was more common than human sacrifice. In it, a person used a stone knife, a stingray spine, or a spine from the maguey—a plant in the agave family— to pierce his or her own skin to draw blood. People most often drew blood from their ears, lips, tongues, or genitals. At times, the person making the autosacrifice would draw a rope, which had knots in it or thorns tied to it, through a hole in his or her tongue, increasing both the pain and the blood loss. Ouch!

The Mesoamericans did not make these sacrifices because they didn't value human blood or life. In fact, the case was quite the opposite. They believed that the blood they spilled was deeply important. It paid their debt to the gods and helped keep the universe in order. These gory sacrifices were

This illustration from Diego Durán's 1579 book *The History of the Indies of New Spain* shows Aztec priests holding down a victim and cutting his heart out during a human sacrifice.

among the shared cultural elements of the various peoples of ancient Mesoamerica. It's important to remember that Mesoamerica—an area that now covers Mexico, Guatemala, Belize, Honduras, and El Salvador—was actually home to multiple civilizations.

While the Olmec were not the first people to live in Mesoamerica, they were the first to develop a complex society there. They lived in the lowlands along the Gulf of Mexico. They were the first Mesoamericans to create a writing system—it used hieroglyphs, or pictures that represent words or syllables—and to develop a complex calendar. They are famous for their sculptures, including massive stone heads. Their society lasted from around 1500 to 300 BCE and influenced all of the Mesoamerican civilizations that followed.

Maya civilization lasted a long time and went through several stages. The Maya lived in the Yucatan Peninsula area. There were several dozen Maya city-states—including Tikal, Copán, Palenque, Chichen Itza, and Calakmul. Over time, different ones rose to or fell from power. The Classic Period of Maya civilization lasted from approximately 200 to 900 CE, while the Post-Classic Period stretched from 900 to the arrival of the Spanish in the early sixteenth century.

When the Spanish arrived to conquer Mesoamerica the dominant civilization in the area was the Aztec. The Aztec capital, Tenochtitlan, stood in the spot where Mexico City now stands—though, at the time, it was an island in the middle of the now-drained Lake Texcoco. The Aztec came to the region around 1325 and became a major power around one hundred years later.

Several civilizations flourished in what is now Mexico between the Olmec and Aztec eras. The Aztec came to power by overthrowing the Toltec, whose capital, Tula, is famous for its massive Temple of Quetzalcoatl. The people of Teotihuacan established their city about 30 miles (48 km) north of present-day Mexico City. They were most powerful between 100 BCE and 650 CE . Other civilizations were based in the present-day Mexican state of Oaxaca. Oaxacan powers included the Zapotec, who were powerful from about 600 to 800 CE , and the Mixtec,

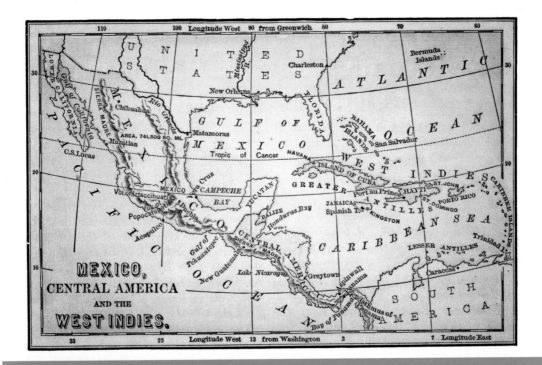

Today, the Mesoamerican region is part of several countries. In the past, it was home to multiple civilizations. Nevertheless, shared cultural elements have united the region in the past and continue to do so today.

who eventually took over the Zapotec stronghold of Monte Albán (which itself was much older than either group).

All of these ancient Mesoamerican civilizations had multi-layered societies, major cities, and a complex religion that featured priests who carried out rituals. And, despite the complexity of the civilizations, their rituals were all very bloody.

CHAPTER ONE

BLOODY SACRIFICES

While the different people of Mesoamerica shared a number of religious practices as well as a similar understanding of how the world worked, they did not all share a single religion. All Mesoamerican religions were polytheistic, which means that believers worshiped a group of gods. However, different groups worshiped different gods. Historians believe that many of the sacrifices in Mesoamerican culture were rituals that acted out central myths—or stories that explain why things are the way they are.

GRUESOME GODS

Mesoamerican art shows us what the ancient Meso-americans thought their gods looked like. To modern eyes, many of them may seem scary and their bodies are disgusting. For example, the Aztec earth goddess Coatlicue wore a skirt made of snakes. Tlaloc—the rain and lightning god who was among the most important Aztec gods—had big, round eyes that are often called "goggle eyes" and fangs like those of a jaguar. The Maya rain god Chac also had fangs and was often shown with goggle eyes. However, what made him recognizable was his long, curving nose. Ah Puch, a Maya death god, was either shown as a skeleton or a bloated corpse. The Aztec and Toltec worshiped Xipe Totec, whose name means "Our Lord the Flayed One." This god of spring, goldsmiths, and newly sprouted plants wore the skin of a human victim. The worship of Quetzalcoatl—known as the "feathered Serpent" because that was what he looked like—dates back at least as far as the people of Teotihuacan. He was also an important god to the Aztec, and while he did not play a role in all Maya states, he was honored under the name Kukulkan in Chichen Itza and several other Post-Classic Maya states.

These drawings of the Aztec gods Huitzilopochtli, Tezcatlipoca, Tlaloc, and Paynal come from a manuscript called the *Florentine Codex*.

The Mesoamericans believed that the gods were very powerful and controlled nature. Rain gods brought the rain, while wind gods cleared the way for rain gods. Corn gods ensured the growth of the corn crop, which was the most important food. The gods were responsible for the movements

WERE-JAGUARS

One of the strangest and most mysterious figures to show up in Mesoamerican art is what scholars call the "were-jaguar." As its name suggests, the were-jaguar was half-human and half-jaguar, "the offspring, according to myth, of a male jaguar and a human woman," or "the result of the mating of a male jaguar and a human woman." Mythological traditions worldwide frequently feature offspring derived from human-divine or human-animal coupling. Yuck! The jaguar is the most powerful predator in Mesoamerica, so jaguars played a big role in Mesoamerican mythology and were an important symbol of strength and power. While gods with jaguarlike features appear in later Mesoamerican cultures, the were-jaguar itself was specifically Olmec. Some historians think that the were-jaguar may have been the main deity, or god, of the Olmec people.

Whatever they were, were-jaguars were really weird looking! Their bodies were plump like a baby's, and they had turned-down mouths with fleshy lips. Their heads were cleft, meaning they looked as though they were cut with a knife or an ax at the top. Some sculptures show a were-jaguar baby being held by a calm man. Because of the way that the men are holding them, people have suggested that the were-jaguar babies are being sacrificed.

of the sun and the moon. They made the soil good for growth. They provided everything necessary for human life. However, these gods were quite demanding. If the gods' favor was lost, they could become angry and vengeful. Hurricanes, droughts, and loss in battle were all attributed to the anger of the gods.

BLOOD AND BONES

Sacrifice played a big role in Mesoamerican stories about the gods. The Aztec creation story illustrates how central sacrifice was to their understanding of the world. The ancient Aztec believed that the world in which they lived was the fifth world that had been created. Just like each of the previous creations, their universe started with the creation of a sun. A humble god threw himself into a sacred fire and became the sun. A proud god hesitated before throwing himself into the fire, and so he became the moon. In order to keep the proud moon from outshining the humble sun, another god threw a rabbit into the moon, dimming it. While a new sun had been created, it could not—or in other versions of the story, would not—move across the sky. To make the sun move, the rest of the gods all sacrificed themselves. The Aztec believed that they needed to make routine human sacrifices to make sure the sun would rise every morning, just as the gods had sacrificed themselves to make the fifth sun begin moving.

The Aztec story of the creation of human beings also features sacrifice. To create humans in this world (the fifth sun), the god Quetzalcoatl traveled to the underworld, Mictlan, to gather up the bones from all the corpses of the people who lived under the previous sun. Despite the efforts of Mictlantecuhtli, the king of the underworld, Quetzalcoatl escaped with their bones. However, during his escape, Quetzalcoatl tripped and broke the bones. The gods then cut themselves, drawing their own blood and sprinkling it over the broken bones. The divine blood brought them to life. The Aztec believed that because people were made from these broken bones, humans come in different shapes and sizes.

IMPRESSIVE TEMPLES, CHILLING RITUALS

Many of the huge stepped pyramids built by the ancient Mesoamericans still stand today. They draw tourists from around the world who marvel at them. Smaller temples have also survived, along with carefully laid out courts and many-roomed palaces. These remains have increased historians' and archaeologists' interest in Mesoamerican history. However, they also hold some gruesome secrets as well as a few remains of the human variety.

Most of the pyramids, smaller temples, and palaces were parts of elaborately planned complexes at the hearts of cities. The rulers of different Mesoamerican cities competed to build the biggest and most impressive complexes. The complexes showed off the power of both the cities in which they were located and the people who ruled those cities.

One of the most impressive complexes was in the city of Teotihuacan. The huge Pyramid of the Moon, the even more massive Pyramid of the Sun, and the Temple of the Feathered Serpent—known for the incredible carvings that decorate it—are the highlights of the monuments along the Avenue of the Dead. While we don't know that the city's original inhabitants called the street by that name—it was the Aztec who, impressed by the monuments, named most of the buildings in Teotihuacan, which was already in ruins by the time they discovered it—it is a fitting one.

Some pyramids were also tombs! This stepped pyramid in the Maya city of Palenque is known as the Temple of Inscriptions. It contains the tomb of the ruler K'ihnich Janaab' Pakal, also known as Pakal the Great.

Archaeologists discovered a number of graves in the Pyramid of the Moon. Each grave held several corpses. One or two of the bodies in each grave seemed to be those of powerful people. These bodies were carefully arranged and had valuable objects with them. However, the rest of the bodies had their hands bound behind their backs and had been tossed into the graves in a less respectful manner. These people had been sacrificed at the time of a powerful leader's burial. In one grave, the heads of the sacrificial victims had been cut off. Archaeologists also found the skeletons of animals that had been sacrificed, including several

TROPHY SKULLS

While the bodies of some sacrificial victims were buried out of sight, there were still plenty of public reminders of human sacrifice in Aztec temples. One of the most gruesome was the *tzompantli*, or skull rack. This was exactly what it sounds like. Each *tzompantli* displayed several rows of severed human heads. Historians have long known about *tzompantlis* from historic accounts; there were also stone carvings that showed what they looked like.

In 2009, archaeologists made a discovery in Mexico City's Plaza Manuel Gamio that gave us a better understanding of how these skull racks were constructed. They found five human skulls with holes drilled into their temples. In Aztec times, the skulls had been stuck on a wooden

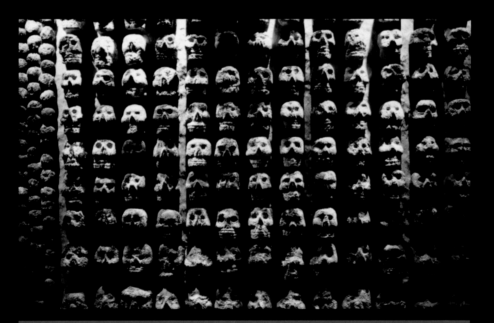

There's no denying that the skulls from this *tzompantli*, excavated in Mexico City, are kind of creepy. Knowing that the skulls came from people who were sacrificed makes it even worse.

stake, much like you might stick several marshmallows on a stick to roast them (although the former does sound far less appetizing). While this may seem like a disrespectful way to treat the dead, there is no reason to assume the Aztec saw it that way. In fact, archaeologists discovered that the skulls had been decorated with cornflowers, cotton blossoms, and cactus thorns.

In the later years of Maya civilization, the Maya used skull racks, too. Before that, however, early Maya rulers wore the decapitated skulls of captives as trophies! Some early Maya rulers were also buried with the decapitated skulls of sacrificed captives.

members of the dog family (either coyotes or wolves), large cats (pumas or jaguars), and birds (including some eagles). Historians believe that the people of Teotihuacan associated all these animals with warriors. These bloody remains were severed and hurled on top of powerful leaders' corpses in sacrificial ceremonies.

The archaeologists excavating the Pyramid of the Moon also found that it had been rebuilt several times. Each new version was built on top of an earlier one. In all, there were seven layers of construction. As it turns out, many of the Mesoamerican pyramids were built up in layers over time. Historians knew that the Templo Mayor, or Great Temple, in the Aztec capital of Tenochtitlan had been destroyed by the Spanish, who used its stones to build the Metropolitan Cathedral of the Assumption of Mary, a major Catholic church.

In the 1980s, archaeologists discovered that several older versions of the Templo Mayor still existed, buried on the spot where the temple once stood. When they began digging on the site, they found a lot of interesting—if not, disturbing—things.

One carved disk they found illustrated the story of how the god Huitzilopochtli murdered his sister Coyolxauhqui and cut up her body after she insulted their pregnant mother. Even grosser, they also found the remains of real human bodies that had been cut up just like Coyolxauhqui and buried at the base of the temple.

Like other Mesoamericans, the Maya used human sacrifice to mark important occasions, such as the naming of a new ruler or the dedication of an important building. In times of drought and famine they made sacrifices to the rain gods.

One of the most famous places where sacrifices happened was the Sacred Cenote at Chichen Itza. Also known as the Well of Sacrifice, the Sacred Cenote was a deep pond, fed by an underground stream. Archaeologists found the remains of at least fifty human victims—men, women, and children—who had been thrown into the well. Precious objects, including masks, jewelry, gold and copper plates, jade and shell beads, and sacrificial knives, were also thrown in as sacrifices. The most common offerings were cakes of incense, some of them still attached to incense burners. Burning incense—made from the resin of the copal tree—was a common method of honoring the gods across Mesoamerica. Incense was burned both in the homes of ordinary people and in temples.

CHAPTER TWO

BRUTAL WARFARE

Historians believe that the main goal of warfare in ancient Mesoamerica was for cities to increase their power and influence. When one city had beaten another, it required a steady stream of tribute from the people it had defeated. Luxury goods—such as exotic bird feathers, jade and other valuable stones, beautifully carved figurines, expensive dyes, finely woven textiles, and cacao beans (which are used to make chocolate)—were one kind of tribute. Captives for sacrifice were another.

A BLOODY TRIBUTE

There were many methods of sacrifice depending on who was doing the sacrificing and what god the victim was being offered to. The Spanish priest Diego de Landa described a Maya sacrifice that took place in the sixteenth century. The victim and the priests who sacrificed him were all painted blue. The victim was taken to the top of the temple platform and made to lie down on a stone there. Then four priests—called *chac*, after the Maya god of sacrifice—held the victim's

FLOWER WARS

While they also engaged in warfare on a larger scale, the Aztec were particularly known for fighting small-scale conflicts called flower wars. These were pre-arranged battles that were fought by small armies. The flower wars benefitted the Aztec in several ways. For one thing, they were a good source of captives for human sacrifice. In fact, historians believe that the Aztec started the flower war tradition in the early 1450s when there was a series of famines, which the Aztec responded to with a steady stream of human sacrifices.

Flower wars were also a good way for the Aztec to intimidate their enemies. They proved a good training ground for young warriors, too. Flower wars allowed the Aztec to keep hostilities with their enemies fresh without committing to the costs and risks of a full-scale war. Some historians believe that they hurt the Aztec in the long run, though. One of the reasons that the Spanish were able to conquer the Aztec so quickly was that many of the Aztec's neighbors were happy to turn on them after years of being subjected to flower wars.

limbs while a fifth priest stabbed the victim in the chest, plunged his hand into the victim's body, and pulled put the still-throbbing heart. The priest put the heart on a plate, and then another priest rubbed blood from it on the idols—or religious statues—nearby.

The Aztec also had at least a dozen different forms of sacrifice. One of the most common was cutting out the heart in a manner much like the Maya sacrifice described by de Landa. After a battle, the first warriors to be captured had a stone tied to one leg and then were forced to fight against better-armed Aztec warriors. Other captives might be tied to a wooden frame and shot full of arrows or burned in a ritual fire.

This illustration from a sixteenth-century manuscript shows prisoners of war being sacrificed to the Aztec sun god. Regular human sacrifices to Huitzilopochtli were important in Aztec religion.

While many human sacrifices were carried out because of unforeseen events (such as battles, floods, or earthquakes), human sacrifices were a routine part of many of the festivals that appeared in each cycle of the Aztec calendar. For example, boys, girls, and deity representatives were sacrificed at daybreak and midday on Huey Tozoztli, a festival in the fourth month of the Aztec calendar. Deity representatives were people—often captives or slaves—who stood in for a particular god or goddess.

After a victim had been killed, the Aztec might do a variety of things with his or her body. Sometimes, especially if the victim had been a warrior, part of the body would be eaten. The victim's head could, of course, be cut off and placed in a *tzompantli*. Victims sacrificed to Xipe Totec had their skin stripped off. The victim's skin would then be draped over a young man representing Xipe Totec, who would take part in other rituals honoring the god. Sometimes the bodies of victims were hurled off of the pyramid-temples where the sacrifices took place in the crowd that had gathered to watch below.

ALTERNATIVE TO WAR: A DEADLY GAME

Are you a fan of ball games? How would you like to play one in which the stakes were life or death? While the games played in the stone ball courts found in almost every Mesoamerican city didn't always end in the deaths of the losing team, they did often enough to make you think twice about playing. There are plenty of images of the players for the losing team getting their heads cut off. There are even images of the game being played with the chopped-off heads of losing players! (Though it seems more likely this was an artist's attempt to symbolically show the stakes of the game than an illustration of how the game was actually played).

We don't know exactly what the rules of the game were. In fact, they may have varied over time and from place to place. However, there are several things about the Mesoamerican ballgame that seem to have remained the same. It was always played on a large, rectangular stone court. Players on opposing teams hit a rubber ball back and forth, trying to keep it always in motion as modern players do in volleyball or tennis. However, players in the Mesoamerican ballgame were only allowed to hit the ball with their hips, thighs, and knees. Hitting the ball with any other body part or failing to pass it to the other side of the ball court resulted in a foul. Some courts had a small stone ring in the center of each wall. While

The Mesoamerican ball game ended in death for many of those who played it. This modern illustration shows people observing the game being played in the ballcourt of the Maya city of Copán.

getting the ball through this hole was very hard, if a player did so his team immediately won the game.

Even for the winning team, the game could be deadly. Serious injuries were common, despite the helmets and thick padding players wore. By the end of a game, players were often bloody and bruised—sometimes so badly that their bruises were cut open to drain the blood. Some players even died from hard hits to the stomach or head. After all, the solid, rubber balls could weigh up to 10 pounds (4.5 kg).

The violent games were popular entertainment. Spectators gathered to watch in large numbers and often made extravagant bets on the outcome of the games. However, the game had ritual meaning, as well. It was sometimes a stand-in for going to war against an enemy. Games were also played as a way to reenact victories, pitting war captives against their conquerors. These games were likely rigged in some way and ended with the members of the losing team getting their heads chopped off.

ALL IN STONE

The ancient Mesoamericans never learned to work with hard metals, such as iron. This means that all of their weapons—for both hunting and warfare—were made out of stone. The kinds of stone that the Mesoamericans used to make weapons were chert, flint, and obsidian, which is a black volcanic glass. Even though they were made of stone, these weapons were still deadly!

Less elite members of the fighting forces used bows and arrows or rocks and slingshots. Warriors used spear-throwers with long

wooden shafts that were tipped with sharp chert or obsidian blades. For fighting in closer quarters, they also carried *macuahuitls*, which have been variously described as a kind of war club or sword. Made of wood, their sides were lined with obsidian blades. They were between 2 and 4 feet long (0.6–1.2 m). According to reports from early Spanish explorers, they were sharp enough to slice the head off of a horse.

The spear-throwers that the ancient Mesoamericans used were called *atlatls*.

IT'S ALL ABOUT THE CAPTIVES

It was a greater mark of prowess for Mesoamerican warriors to capture enemy soldiers in battle than to just kill them outright. Captives would prove useful as sacrifices, after all. While warriors were captured during battle, women and children would be taken captive after their cities were defeated. The Aztec made use of the fact that nose piercing was a common practice by stringing their captives together by cords that ran through the holes in their noses. That had to hurt!

Human sacrifice wasn't the only terrible fate captives faced. Maya rulers were known to publicly torture captives from enemy city-states. Prisoners might be dragged around by the hair, have the tips of their fingers cut off, have their fingernails torn out, or be forced to let blood.

Aztec warriors gained admission to elite warrior societies based on how many enemy warriors they had captured. Warriors who had captured at least four captives could become jaguar warriors or eagle warriors. While jaguar warriors wore jaguar skins, eagle knights wore helmets

This statue of an eagle warrior was found during the excavation of Tenochtitlán's Templo Mayor.

that looked like the open beak of an eagle. The highest-level warrior society was the Cuachicqueh, or "shorn ones." They shaved off all their hair except a braid over their left ears and painted their faces half red and half blue or yellow. They swore to always push forward in battle and to kill any other member of their society who took a step back. That's the kind of extreme group you might just regret joining!

CHAPTER THREE

DAILY LIFE

While the centrality of sacrifice in ancient Mesoamerica would probably be the main reason you wouldn't want to live there, there were plenty of aspects of daily life that modern people would definitely find strange, and maybe even a bit stomach turning. For example, standards of beauty and cleanliness differ from culture to culture, and some Mesoamericans gave truth to the saying, "Beauty kills."

YOU CALL THAT BEAUTIFUL?

Both the Olmec and the Maya engaged in a practice called cranial deformation, or the deliberate reshaping of people's skulls. The Olmec bound babies' heads to make them longer, while the Maya would strap boards to the front and back of a baby's head to achieve the flattened foreheads they found so attractive. The Maya also considered crossed eyes beautiful. Mothers would hang a bead in front of a baby's eyes in the hopes that the baby would grow up into a lovely cross-eyed adult. Maya leaders were often depicted with elongated foreheads or noses, intentionally narrow eyes, and other deformed features.

While modern people value a mouthful of shining white teeth, the ancient Mesoamericans had different ideals. They actually had good dental health, thanks to polishing their teeth with salt and charcoal and occasionally using unsweetened chewing gum. However, Aztec women also used a dye made out of ground-up cochineal beetles to dye their teeth red, as that was considered beautiful. (The same red dye made from this beetle is still used as a food coloring for many juices and snacks today!) Members of the Maya elite would file their teeth and inlay, or set, precious stones in them.

Piercings—especially of the ears, lips, and septum of the nose—were very common among the Mesoamericans. The Mixtec, Olmec, Aztec, and Maya were all partial to plugs that created large holes in their ears. Depending on where you live, you might know some modern-day friends with these kinds of piercings, too. These kinds of body modifications, or changes, are a style people tend to have strong opinions

Every society has its own idea of beauty. This head from Palenque shows the long forehead and crossed eyes that the Maya found attractive.

about. You either love the look of them or think they're really ugly. That fact alone is a reminder that beauty is very much in the eye of the beholder.

KEEPING CLEAN

The ancient Mesoamericans placed a high value on cleanliness. They disliked filth and bad smells. The copal incense they burned during religious rituals helped cover up the smell of the decomposing bodies that those rituals produced. Spanish sources say that the Aztec planted aromatic, or sweet-smelling, trees around Tenochtitlan to make the surrounding air smell sweet. They also reportedly collected human excrement and carted it away for use in fertilizer, salt making, and tanning (or leather making). This may sound gross, but it meant that human waste wasn't just sitting around in the streets.

Steam baths were common across Mesoamerica. Both the elite and the common people had access to them. They were generally small, domed

There were strict rules about who could wear what in Aztec society. Noblemen, like the one in this modern drawing, wore a lot of exotic feathers and piercings.

buildings with a vent at the top, a central firebox, a small door, and a bench around the room. Steam baths kept the ancient Mesoamericans pretty clean. However, they didn't offer much privacy! Bathers had to share the same room with the rest of their family, and maybe even a few neighbors, too.

While the Spanish were impressed by the cleanliness of most of the Mesoamerican peoples they encountered, they were grossed

AZTEC SCHOOLS

There were two kinds of Aztec schools, the *calmecac* and the *telpochcalli*. The *calmecac* was the school for children of the elite class, though some commoners were admitted as well. While both boys and girls attended the *calmecac*, only boys are known to have lived on the school grounds. Religious training was the main focus of education there, and it was where all priests, judges, and other high officials were trained. Students also learned reading, writing, and how to read and understand the complex Aztec calendar.

The *telpochcalli* was the school that most children of commoners attended, though there were a few children from the elite class whose parents chose to send them here as well. Students here learned similar things to those at the *calmecac*, but with a greater emphasis on military training, trade skills, and homemaking skills.

All young people—but especially those attending the *calmecac*—faced painful punishments if they misbehaved. This included being pricked with spines from the maguey plant, being beaten with nettle switches, and being forced to breathe in the smoke from burning chili peppers.

out by the Aztec priests. This is because Aztec priests were not allowed to bathe. As a result, they were covered in dried blood from the routine human sacrifices and the autosacrifices that they performed. Their hair was matted with it, their clothes were caked in it, and they smelled horrible.

HOME SWEET HOME

How would you like to live in a house where dead bodies were buried? It may sound creepy to you, but it was normal among the Maya. While members of the elite class were often buried in fancy tombs, the common people were usually buried under the floors of their family home. The bodies of babies and young children

Compared to the houses that most people live in today, the houses that ordinary ancient Mesoamericans lived in were small, cramped, and uncomfortable.

who had died early were often placed in a large urn before being buried.

Houses throughout Mesoamerica were generally built of adobe, or sun-dried mud, bricks or of mud spread over a framework of lashed-together plants. The houses of ordinary people tended to be small, consisting of one room where the whole family slept. Kitchens tended to be small separate buildings, as did steam baths. The members of an extended family might share the same kitchen and steam bath.

ARE YOU SURE THAT WILL CURE ME?

The ancient Mesoamericans believed that illness and injury were results of either disapproval of the gods, magic, or natural causes. As a result, they treated sickness and injury in a mix of ways. A broken bone would be put in a cast or splint, but a prayer would also be said over it.

Mesoamerican healers used a lot of unusual herbs, roots, and other plants in their cures. One Aztec treatment for dandruff was to wash your head with urine, rub a powder made from avocado pits into your scalp, and then apply *yiamolli* (or red inkplant) leaves to your head. Urine was also used to clean wounds. For a headache, the Aztec prescribed breathing in green tobacco. (Now, of course, we know that tobacco is bad for you!) If a headache got worse, the patient would be told to take a powder made from the *cocoyatic* plant. If that didn't do the trick either, the healer would use an obsidian blade to bleed the person. The Aztec also believed that to avoid tooth infections, a person could rub powdered charcoal on his or her teeth, and rinse them with salt and urine.

de las yeruas medicinales. fo. 142.

This description of plants used in Mesoamerican medicine is from the *Florentine Codex.* This manuscript, compiled by the Spaniard Bernardino de Sahagún, used the work of Mesoamerican artists.

Healers knew not only which plants would cure disease, but also which ones were hallucinogenic, or able to bring about an altered state of mind in people. These included the peyote cactus and a kind of mushroom known as the *teonanácatl*. These plants had a legitimate place in Mesoamerican religion, and they are still used in rituals by Mesoamericans today, as well as some Native Americans from the American Southwest. However, the plants are banned as illegal drugs in many countries, including the United States (though there is an exemption for use among certain Native American groups).

CHAPTER FOUR

TIME TO EAT!

Different cultures have different foods, and what people like is often a matter of what they are used to. As you might imagine, some of the foods the ancient Mesoamericans ate are things that we enjoy today, while others are things that would seem pretty disgusting to most of us.

CORN, WONDERFUL CORN!

The staple, or main, food of the Mesoamerican diet was—and still is—corn. Corn, which is also known as maize, was first domesticated in Mesoamerica. Corn deities are important in Mesoamerican religion. For example, the father of the Hero Twins in the Maya creation story is the corn god.

As you might guess from the crown of corncobs he is wearing, this alarming figure is a corn god. The statue comes from Oaxaca.

32

After it was harvested, corn was usually dried. Not long before it was time to eat the corn, the kernels would be pulled off the cob. Then they would be soaked in a mix of water and either ash or lime (used for their chemicals calcium hydroxide and potassium hydroxide). While this may sound unappetizing, it actually made the corn more nutritious. The corn was then ground on a large stone, now known as a metate.

This prepared ground corn was served in several ways. Sometimes it was made into a kind of gruel or porridge. It was also used to make tortillas. These round, thin flat breads (yup, they are same thing that you get in Mexican restaurants today) were cooked on a stone griddle. Corn was also used to make tamales (another name that probably rings a bell), which were stuffed with fillings such as beans or chili peppers, wrapped in cornhusks, and boiled in water.

OTHER MESOAMERICAN CROPS

Along with corn, the Mesoamericans ate a lot of squash and beans. They also ate tomatoes, avocados, sweet potatoes, papayas, breadfruit, amaranth, and prickly pear cacti. Several kinds of chili peppers were used to flavor foods. Other foods sound less appetizing. For instance, the Aztec ate cakes of blue-green algae that the Spanish conquistador Bernal Díaz del Castillo said tasted like cheese!

Depending on the landscape, different farming methods were used. In jungle areas, the Maya used the slash-and-burn method to clear land. This method means forests were cut down and the brush burned to make way for fields. Then Maya farmers would use a digging stick to make holes to drop seeds into. Avocado, breadfruit, and papaya trees could be grown along the forest edge. The Aztec are famous for their chinampas. They built rectangular, manmade islands on which crops were grown in the shallow waters of Lake Texcoco. The Mesoamericans often used human excrement as fertilizer. While that sounds pretty gross, it actually did make for richer soil! Every crop grew tall and strong thanks to the nutrients it got from human poop.

This painting shows the construction of a chinampa. Once the fields were built up, human poop helped fertilize them. Gross as it sounds, people in cultures around the world have used poop for fertilizer.

DUCK, DUCK... DOG?

The Mesoamericans had few domesticated animals. However, they did raise turkeys, ducks, and dogs. Like they do today, turkeys and ducks provided both eggs and meat. While the Mesoamericans raised some dogs as hunting dogs, guard dogs, or pets, they also raised dogs—particularly small, hairless dogs—for food. The idea of eating a dog may seem repulsive to you, but which animals are considered acceptable for eating varies a lot from culture to culture. Even today, dog meat is still eaten in many parts of China, Korea, and Vietnam, as well as in some countries in Africa.

Ancient Mesoamericans hunted and fished for wild animals. Along with deer, rabbits, and wild members of the pig family called peccaries, the Maya also hunted less tasty-sounding critters, such as armadillos and monkeys. The Aztec enjoyed eating iguana. They caught not only fish, but also frogs, tadpoles, and newts such as the axolotl from Lake Texcoco.

How do you feel about creepy crawlers working their way down to your stomach? Bugs, including ants, grasshoppers, and maguey worms, also had a place in their diet. A popular staple of the Aztec diet that is still eaten in certain regions of Mexico today were *chapulines*. These grasshoppers were available in large quantities. Even today they are fried and added to eggs, tacos, and other common Mexican foods. *Azcamolli* (modern Spanish *escamoles*) were the name for the larvae and pupae of *Liometopum apiculatum*. For those of you who don't know scientific classifications, that's ant! The Aztec name for the dish in Nahuatl means "ant stew." Just like grasshopper, these ant dishes are still widely

CHOCOLATE

Did you know that chocolate comes from Mesoamerica? Chocolate is made from the beans of the cacao tree. However, the kind of chocolate you would have found in ancient Mesoamerica wasn't the sweet treat that people around the world enjoy today. The Mesoamericans prepared a frothy drink made out of ground-up cacao beans and water. The Aztec called this drink *xocolatl*, which, as you might have guessed, is the source of the English word "chocolate." Unless it is sweetened, chocolate is actually very bitter. To cut the bitterness, vanilla, honey, or chili powder were added to the drink.

Chocolate was a luxury food and was drunk mainly by the elites. Cacao beans were also a valuable trade item and even ended up becoming a form of currency!

This image of a native Mexican making a chocolate drink is from a sixteenth-century manuscript called the *Codex Tudela*.

consumed in certain regions of Mexico today. These edible insects might not appeal to you, but they were a good source of protein in the Aztec diet!

At one point, historians argued that the Aztec practiced cannibalism because they lacked protein in their diets. We now know that's not true. The Aztecs ate plenty of protein, and cannibalism happened only on a small scale and only as a part of certain religious rituals. Still this misunderstanding reminds us how hard it can be to understand why people in foreign or past cultures do things differently from us. After all, there are certainly things about our own culture that the ancient Mesoamericans would have found weird. There are probably even some that they would have found gross!

All these weird foods, bloody sacrifices, and bizarre living habits may seem out of place to you. But remember that they're just cultural differences. Mesoamerican civilizations, especially the Maya and the Aztec, created lasting cultural contributions. Their influence is still felt in the traditional arts, foods, and religious practices of Central America. Their culture—even its grosser elements—ought to be celebrated.

GLOSSARY

amaranth A kind of plant that is grown for its grains.

archaeologist A scientist who studies the remains and artifacts of past cultures.

cannibalism The practice of eating other human beings.

civilization A society with a high level of organization and development.

complex A group of buildings with a related purpose.

conquistador One of the Spanish soldiers who conquered civilizations in the Americas.

culture A group of people with shared customs, traditions, and beliefs.

currency The system of money in a country.

deity A god or goddess.

domesticate To tame animals for livestock or raise plants as crops.

elite The social group with the most power and privilege.

famine A period during which there is not enough food to eat.

fertilizer A substance used to make crops grow better.

Nahuatl The language of the Aztec people.

protein Organic molecules found in foods such as eggs, milk, meat, and beans that is necessary for the human diet.

ritual A religious ceremony that is done in a certain, symbolic way.

textile A type of cloth or fabric.

tribute Goods or other forms of taxes demanded by a powerful ruler.

FOR MORE INFORMATION

American Museum of Natural History
Central Park West at 79th Street
New York, NY 10024
(212) 769-5100
Website: http://www.amnh.org
Since it was founded in 1896, this museum has worked to
    advance the public knowledge of world cultures and the
    natural world. It has a great collection of Mesoamerican
    archaeological finds.

The Field Museum
1400 South Lake Shore Drive
Chicago, IL 60605
(312) 922-9410
Website: http://www.fieldmuseum.org
This natural history museum has an excellent Mesoamerican
    and Central American collection. Visitors will learn about
    the sciences of archaeology and anthropology as well as
    Mesoamerican history.

The Gardiner Museum
111 Queen's Park
Toronto, ON M5S 2C7
Canada
(416) 586-8080
Website:
Canada's national ceramics museum holds an interesting collec-
    tion of ancient American ceramics. It also offers classes for
    anyone interested in learning how ceramics are made.

Institute for Mesoamerican Studies
Arts & Sciences, 233
1400 Washington Avenue
Albany, NY 12222
Website: http://www.albany.edu/ims/index.html
Associates of this institute have carried out archaeological,
    ethnographic, and linguistic studies of Mesoamerica. It
    also has an impressive collection of Mesoamerican textiles.

The Mesoamerica Center
Department of Art and Art History
University of Texas At Austin: College of Fine Arts
2301 Trinity Street
Austin, TX 78712
(512) 471–3382
Website: https://www.utexas.edu/finearts/aah/about
    /research-centers/mesoamerica-center
This interdisciplinary organization aims to promote the study
    of Mesoamerican languages, arts, and archaeology. It also
    operates the Casa Herrera research and teaching center in
    Antigua, Guatemala.

The National Museum of Anthropology
Avenida Paseo de la Reforma y Calzada Gandhi s/n
Chapultepec Polanco, Miguel Hidalgo
11560 Ciudad de México, DF
Mexico
+52 55 4040 5300
Website: http://www.mna.inah.gob.mx/index.html

Mexico's most visited museum has a whole wealth of information about Mexican history before the Spanish conquest. While the museum's website is in Spanish, it has great images of some of the museum's key artifacts.

WEBSITES

Because of the changing nature of Internet links, Rosen Publishing has developed an online list of websites related to the subject of this book. This site is updated regularly. Please use this link to access this list:

http://www.rosenlinks.com/TGH/Meso

FOR FURTHER READING

Burgan, Michael. *Ancient Aztecs* (Ancient World). New York, NY: Children's Press, 2012.

Doeden, Matt. *Tools and Treasures of the Ancient Maya* (Searchlight Books—What Can We Learn from Early Civilizations?) Minneapolis, MN: Lerner Publishing Group, 2014.

Frydenborg, Kay. *Chocolate: Sweet Science & Dark Secrets of the World's Favorite Treat*. New York, NY: HMH Books for Young Readers, 2015.

Grove, David C. *Discovering the Olmecs: An Unconventional History*. Austin, TX: University of Texas Press, 2014.

Holm, Kirsten. *Everyday Life in the Maya Civilization* (Jr. Graphic Ancient Civilizations). New York, NY: PowerKids Press, 2012.

Hunter, Nick. *Daily Life in the Maya Civilization* (Infosearch: Daily Life in Ancient Civilizations). Mankato, MN: Heinemann-Raintree, 2015.

Kuiper, Kathleen. *Pre-Columbian America: Empires of the New World* (The Britannica Guide to Ancient Civilizations). New York, NY: Rosen Educational Publishing, 2010.

Lowe, Lindsey. *Ancient Aztec and Maya* (Facts at Your Fingertips). London, United Kingdom: Brown Bear Books, 2009.

Mann, Charles C. *1491: New Revelations of the Americas Before Columbus*. New York, NY: Vinatage Books, 2006.

Mundy, Barbara E. *The Death of Aztec Tenochtitlan, the Life of Mexico City*. Austin, TX: University of Texas Press, 2015.

Pipe, Jim. *Mysteries of the Mayan Calendar*. New York, NY: Crabtree Publishing, 2013.

Quilter, Jeffrey. *The Civilization of the Incas* (Illustrated History of the Ancient World). New York, NY: Rosen Publishing, 2012.

Raum, Elizabeth. *What Did the Aztecs Do for Me?* (Linking the Past and Present). Mankato, MN: Heinemann-Raintree, 2010.

Tedlock, Dennis. *Popol Vuh: The Definitive Edition of The Mayan Book of The Dawn of Life and The Glories of Gods and Kings*. New York, NY: Touchstone, 1996.

Somervill, Barbara A. *Ancient Maya* (The Ancient World). New York, NY: Children's Press, 2012.

BIBLIOGRAPHY

Aguilar-Moreno, Manuel. *Handbook to Life in the Aztec World*. New York, NY: Facts on File, 2006.

Albert R. Mann Library. "Chocolate: Food of the Gods." Cornell University. Retrieved August 27, 2015 (http://exhibits.mannlib.cornell.edu/chocolate/index.php).

Atwood, Roger. "Under Mexico City." *Archaeology*, June 9, 2014. Retrieved August 13, 2015 (http://www.archaeology.org/issues/138-1407/features/2173-mexico-city-aztec-buried-world).

Baquedano, Elizabeth. *Aztec, Inca & Maya*. Revised Edition. New York, NY: DK, 2011.

Coe, Michael D., and Rex Koontz. *Mexico: From the Olmecs to the Aztecs*. Reprint Edition. New York, NY: Thames & Hudson, 2004.

Dils, Lorna. "Aztec Mythology." Yale-New Haven Teachers Institute. Retrieved August 14, 2015 (http://www.yale.edu/ynhti/curriculum/units/1994/3/94.03.03.x.html).

Evans, C.T. "Mesoamerican Civilization" *Nova Online*, May 7, 2012. Retrieved August 9, 2015 (http://novaonline.nvcc.edu/eli/evans/his111/notes/mesoamerica.html).

Feinman, Gary M., Linda M. Nicholas, and Helen R. Haines. "Mexico's Wonder Plant." *Archaeology*, 55, no. 5 (September/October 2002). Retrieved August 13, 2015 (http://archive.archaeology.org/0209/abstracts/mexico.html).

Harvey, H.R. "Public Health in Aztec Society." *Bulletin of the New York Academy of Medicine*, 57, no. 2 (March 1981): 157–165. Retrieved August 27, 2015 (http://www.ncbi.nlm.nih.gov/pmc/articles/PMC1805201/?page=1).

Hathaway, James. "Defining Teotihuacan: Findings Shed New Light on Ancient City." Arizona State University. Retrieved

August 13, 2015 (http://www.asu.edu/feature/fall04
/teotihuacan.html).

Hearn, Kelly. "Who Built the Great City of Teotihuacan?"
National Geographic. Retrieved August 9, 2015. (http://
science.nationalgeographic.com/science/archaeology
/teotihuacan-/).

Heilbrunn Timeline of Art History. "Tenochtitlan." The Metropolitan Museum of Art. Retrieved August 15, 2015 (http://
www.metmuseum.org/toah/hd/teno_1/hd_teno_1.htm).

Perl, Lila. *The Ancient Maya*. New York, NY: Scholastic, 2005.

Petrus, Monica. "The Brutal and Bloody History of the Mesoamerican Ball Game, Where Sometimes Loss Was Death."
Atlas Obscura, January 9, 2013. Retrieved August 20, 2015
(http://www.atlasobscura.com/articles/meso-american
-baseball).

Sharer, Robert J. *Daily Life in Maya Civilization*. Second Edition.
Westport, CT: Greenwood Press, 2009.

Smith, Michael E. "Aztecs." in *Oxford Handbook of the Archaeology
of Ritual and Religion*, edited by Timothy Insoll, pp. 555–569.
Oxford, U.K.: Oxford University Press, 2011. Retrieved August
12, 2015 (http://www.public.asu.edu/~mesmith9/1
-CompleteSet/MES-11-AztecRitual.pdf).

Smithsonian. "Olmec Legacy." Smithsonian Institution. Retrieved
August 20, 2015 (http://anthropology.si.edu/olmec/english/).

UNESCO World Heritage Centre. "Historic Centre of Oaxaca
and Archaeological Site of Monte Albán." United Nations.
Retrieved August 9, 2015 (http://whc.unesco.org/en/list/415).

INDEX

ABOUT THE AUTHOR

Abbie Mercer has a long-standing interest in history and has been fascinated with ancient Mesoamerican societies since studying the Maya in middle school. She has written several books for young readers, including *Happy Thanksgiving* and *Goats on a Farm*.

PHOTO CREDITS